blank page

I0407346

blank page

blank page

blank page

blank page

blank page

blank page

blank page

blank page

blank page

blank page

blank page

blank page

blank page

blank page

blank page

blank page

blank page

blank page

blank page

blank page

blank page

blank page

blank page

blank page

blank page

blank page

blank page

blank page

blank page

blank page

blank page

blank page

blank page

blank page

blank page

blank page

blank page

blank page

blank page

blank page

blank page

blank page

blank page

blank page

blank page

blank page

blank page

blank page

blank page

blank page

blank page

blank page

blank page

blank page

blank page

blank page

blank page

blank page

blank page

blank page

blank page

blank page

blank page

blank page

blank page

blank page

blank page

blank page